Interaction Activities in ESL

Pitt Series in English as a Second Language
Beginning and Intermediate Level

Interaction Activities in ESL

Second Edition

Judith Carl Hendrick

Marilyn Smith Butler

Ann Arbor

THE UNIVERSITY OF MICHIGAN PRESS

2000   1999   1998   1997   7   6   5   4

Library of Congress Catalog Card No. 91-66905
ISBN 0-472-08169-1

Illustrations by Neil McCarthy

Foreword to the Second Edition

This is an updated and expanded edition of Judith Carl Kettering's *Interaction Activities in ESL*, which first appeared in 1975 as part of our pioneering attempts to introduce communication activities into the curriculum. The objective remains the same: to help native speakers of other languages develop communicative competence in English. By communicative competence we mean not only knowledge of the linguistic forms but also a knowledge of when, how, and to whom it is appropriate to use these forms. The instructor should explore with the class the speech acts and speech situations from a cross-cultural perspective.

Marilyn Smith Butler has updated the text, adding information and exercises on telephone answering machines, convenience stores, banking machines, and other facets of our changing modern world, including updating the prices (i.e., increasing them). Many new exercises and practice situations have been added, including information gap and information sharing activities in the chapter on community-oriented activities and in the problem solving chapter. Judith Carl Hendrick has added cross-cultural content, particularly in chapter 1. The book remains a text that is intended to provide fun as well as knowledge in the classroom.

Christina Bratt Paulson
Director, English Language Institute
University of Pittsburgh

Contents

Introduction

To the Student

The activities in the first chapter of this book will help you learn some of the speaking rules of social situations and some of the cultural content behind them. In your language you speak differently to a good friend than to a professor, to your younger sister than to your father, etc. Also, in your own language there are phrases you use to greet someone or say goodbye. There are rules for how you introduce people to each other and in what order you introduce them. These are the types of social rules or formulas you will be learning in English in these activities.

The community-oriented projects in the second chapter are designed to encourage you to discover information about your community as well as to give you a chance to talk to native speakers in a structured, focused manner.

Finally, the activities in the problem solving chapter will give you a chance to express your opinions, disagree with your classmates, and compromise. In addition to providing you with this speaking practice, the situations may reveal interesting cultural patterns from both the United States and your home country.

To the Teacher

These materials were developed at the English Language Institute, University of Pittsburgh, for elementary and intermediate students (0–65 score on the Michigan Test of English Language Proficiency) in an intensive program of English as a second language. The activities are designed to help the students make the transition from structured drills to use of English in real-life situations. Creative use of a language involves knowing not only the linguistic forms but also how, when, and to whom the use of these forms is appropriate; therefore, the activities introduce rules of speaking in social situations. The activities give the student a chance to experiment with language forms in which the focus is on meaning rather than on grammatical exactness.

The activities are divided into three major categories according to the type of interaction that is being emphasized. The categories are based on a typology developed by Wilga Rivers ("Talking off the Tops of Their Heads," *TESOL Quarterly,* March 1972) but have been adapted considerably to fit the purposes of these particular materials. The description, purpose, and procedures for use for each group of activities follow.

Social Relations Skill through Conversations

Description and Purpose. Designed for in-class use, these activities provide opportunities for practicing common social expressions which are formulaic and easily memorized; for example, greetings, partings, introductions, complaints, congratulations. The students learn these common expressions and the rules for their use in both formal and informal situations, then practice the expressions in both written form and decreasingly controlled spoken situations.

Procedure for Use. The activities in this chapter should be assigned in the order in which they appear in the book, since the language in the units increases in difficulty as the chapter progresses.

Sections I and II: Dialogues and Analysis

a. Assign the students to read and think about these dialogues the night before you plan to do them in class. Ask them to go over the questions in the analysis section and to try to decide if the dialogues are formal or informal.

b. In class the next day, discuss the dialogues, going over new vocabulary and concepts. Answer and discuss the analysis questions, encouraging cross-cultural discussion as well as focusing on whether each dialogue is formal or informal and what the determining factors are. Point out how the formal/informal distinction is reflected in the language used, eliciting as much information as possible from the students. Perhaps make a chart on the board of the forms and their usage.

Section III: Phrases

a. Build on the phrases already identified in the previous discussion, and complete the picture with those in the book. Model the expressions, explaining the meaning of those that students do not understand and pointing out the formal/

informal distinction. The phrases are written in standard orthography, but one modeling of the expressions should be done in colloquial conversational style and the differences pointed out to the students; for example, How are you doing? (How ya doin'?), I've got to go (I gotta go). These shortened forms should be taught only for recognition because students with low proficiency will mix the styles and sound very peculiar to native speakers.

b. Have the students repeat the expressions together, then individually, using formal style. Pronunciation, stress, and intonation mistakes should be corrected.

Section I: Dialogue Practice

Return to the dialogue section and practice the dialogues.

a. Model the first dialogue for the students and have them repeat it together, with emphasis on correct pronunciation, intonation, and stress.

b. Ask two students to read the dialogue for the class, using the read-and-look-up technique. For this technique, assign roles and have the students face each other. The student reading role A reads the first sentence silently at least once, then looks up at the other student and says it from memory. The student with role B repeats the process with the next sentence, and so on through the dialogue. If the sentence is long, it can be broken up into phrases or clauses. The students will probably try to read aloud from the text at first; it will take some training to get them to look up before speaking. The read-and-look-up technique is well worth the effort, however. The technique, though very simple, is effective in improving pronunciation, intonation, and stress patterns as well as in increasing short-term memory. It also makes the dialogues seem more like real conversations.

Then, have the students practice the dialogue in pairs by themselves for a minute or two before doing the read-and-look-up technique in pairs for the class. Tell the students to read the dialogue to each other quietly. When they finish, they should reverse roles and do the dialogue a second time. This technique requires more time, but it is not time wasted. First, all the students have more opportunity to practice the dialogue, and second, some of the students become so familiar with the dialogue that when they do the read-and-look-up technique for the class, they need only glance at their books once or twice during the performance of the dialogue. We have also found that the additional practice seems to facilitate better transfer of the material to usage outside the classroom.

c. Have the students practice the rest of the dialogues using the same procedures.

Section IV: Practice

a. Written Practice. This section is designed for written, in-class work in pairs or by individuals. The exercises gradually increase in difficulty as the book progresses, from asking the students to simply write a response to a statement to asking them to construct an entire dialogue. In each case, students are always asked to identify the situation as formal or informal. Teachers can collect and correct this work or, even more effectively, have students exchange papers and correct each others' work.

b. Situations. These should be treated as short roleplays in which the students act out the situation. Encourage creativity and improvisation on the basic theme. If some of the situations are inappropriate to your class, revise them to fit your students' surroundings and/or interests. For example, university settings and topics are probably not relevant to a class of refugees. If students seem hesitant to speak at first, you can take one of the roles yourself, thereby directing the course of the roleplay and guiding the student into each exchange. A relaxed atmosphere and a spirit of fun are the keys to the success of these activities. Students need to feel encouraged to speak regardless of errors. In fact, errors are best ignored at this stage unless they lead to a misunderstanding of the message.

Community-Oriented Projects

Description and Purpose. This group of activities is designed primarily for learning outside the classroom. The information that the students gather from these activities (banking, shopping, etc.) is immediately applicable to their everyday lives. The assignments cover such topics as transportation, local entertainment, the supermarket, and university facilities. Each assignment consists of a set of questions designed to elicit both general and specific information. In order to find the answers to the questions, the students must go out into the community or make telephone calls and ask many questions, thereby gaining useful information and communicating in English with people who aren't careful about how fast they speak or what vocabulary they use.

Procedure for Use. These assignments can be done either by groups of students or by individuals. With groups, you may either assign each student a set number of questions or let the group itself decide how to divide up the assignment. In the latter case, each student must understand fully his or her responsibility for obtaining the information. Several of the assignments have comparative exercises, where students should be divided into groups or pairs to collect information on different banks or stores.[1]

After a reasonable amount of time for collecting the information has elapsed (two or three days in an intensive program), set aside part of a class period—at least thirty minutes—for reports and discussion of the collected information. The reports can be given by one or two students from each group as an informal speech which can be tape recorded. At a later time you can meet with the student to listen to the tape and correct pronunciation and grammar errors. Another way to report the information is in an informal discussion, with each student reporting on one or two questions. A circular or semicircular seating arrangement is helpful for this type of discussion. For the comparative exercises, the information sharing can be done in pairs, small groups, or as a class.

We have found that students enjoy these activities but get tired of them if assigned too often. Choose only the units most interesting to your class (or let them choose) and space the units at least two weeks apart.

Problem Solving and Compromising

Description and Purpose. These activities are designed for small-group interaction in problem solving. Each activity consists of a problem for which the students in each group try to reach a unanimous solution. There are usually no "correct answers"; the objective is to get the students into a discussion, each student trying to justify one solution to the problem and persuade the rest of the group to agree. The topics are designed to elicit various cultural attitudes and can serve to stimulate discussion on cross-cultural patterns, if the students' English proficiency is high enough. These activities should not be used at the beginning of instruction with classes of very low proficiency (Michigan Test score 1–40); they should be postponed until students know enough English to be able to discuss the problems, at least at an elementary level (in our experience, from four to six weeks).

Procedure for Use. Divide the class into groups of three or four students. If the group is much larger, some students will cease to take an active role in the discussion.

The day before you plan to use a problem, go over vocabulary in class, and assign students to read it and choose a solution at home as homework. The next day

---

1. For a few items in these assignments you may need to substitute local names for names that are specific to Pittsburgh, Pennsylvania.

in class within their groups, each student discusses his or her choice in turn. The students discuss the solutions until they come to an agreement on one solution—or come to a stalemate. Finally, the class meets as a whole and discusses the various solutions. Each group must be able to justify its solution. Usually the whole activity lasts from fifteen to twenty minutes but may continue longer.

The teacher must be alert during the discussions to point out how various solutions reflect various cultural patterns and values and be prepared to explain the American point of view while still honoring other perspectives.

Chapter 1

Social Relations Skill through Conversations

Greetings

I. Dialogues

1. Jose is a graduate student in Dr. Martin's department. He was in one of Dr. Martin's classes last semester. They meet while waiting for the elevator one morning.

Jose:	Hello, Dr. Martin.
Dr. Martin:	Hello, Jose. How are you?
Jose:	Fine, thank you. And yourself?
Dr. Martin:	Very well, thank you. How is your wife?
Jose:	Oh, she's a little homesick.
Dr. Martin:	That's too bad.

2. Joe and Sam went to the same high school together and are now at the same college. They meet walking across campus.

Sam: Hi, Joe.
Joe: Hi, Sam. How's it going?
Sam: OK. How about you?
Joe: Not bad. By the way, how's your girlfriend?
Sam: Really homesick.
Joe: Too bad!

3. Mayumi and Ms. Freeman meet at the student union café. Ms. Freeman is a foreign student advisor and has helped Mayumi several times with visa problems.

Ms. Freeman: Good morning, Mayumi.
Mayumi: Oh, good morning, Ms. Freeman. How are you?
Ms. Freeman: I'm fine, thank you. I'm enjoying this weather.
Mayumi: Yes, so am I.

4. Linda and Judy used to be roommates and still see each other often. Now they are meeting in one of the classes they take together.

Judy: Hi, Linda.
Linda: Hi, Judy. How are you doing?
Judy: Not so good. I have a cold.
Linda: That's too bad. I hope you feel better soon.

II. Analysis

1. Which dialogues are more formal? Less formal?
2. Usually when someone says, "How are you?" they expect you to say, "Fine." If you don't feel well, answer truthfully only to close friends. If they continue to show interest, it may be all right to give details.
3. "Not bad" = good, and is a positive response.
   "Not so good" = poor, and is a negative response.
4. Would you ask about someone's wife in your culture? Explain.
5. Is weather a common topic of conversation in your country? What are several topics used in your culture with people you may not know very well?
6. Do the greetings in these dialogues seem complete to you, or does your culture demand longer ones? Please explain.

III. Phrases

Formal

Greetings   *Response*

1. Hello Dr./Mr./Ms. *last name.*   Hello.
2. Good Morning Dr./Mr./Ms. *last name.*   Good Morning.
3. How are you?   {Fine, thank you.
                                            {Not very well.

Informal

1. Hi, *first name.*   Hi, *first name.*
                                            {Fine.
                                            {OK.
2. How's it going?   {All right.
   How are you doing?   {Pretty good.
   How are you?   {Not bad.
                                            {Not so good.
                                            {Not much.
3. What's up?   {Nothing special...
   What's new?   {I...

Can you add any to these?

IV. Practice

A. Write a response. Label each F (formal) or I (informal).

   1. Hi, John. I heard you were sick last week.

   2. Good evening, Dr. Thacker. It's nice to see you tonight.

   3. Hi, Peggy! What's new?

   4. Hello, Dr. Miller. How are you today?

B. Situations

   1. It's 9:00 A.M. Greet Mrs. Thomas, who is going to give you a test today.

2. Greet your friend, Maged, and ask him about the party you both went to last night.

3. Greet Mona, who has been sick for several days.

4. Greet Dr. Anthony, a professor in your department. He invited you to his home last week.

5. It's 11:00 at night and you are in the library. You see Takeshi, who was in a class with you last term.

6. Greet your neighbor, Mr. Barnes, at the bus stop. You don't see him very often.

7. Greet Jane, a good friend. You have not seen her for several weeks.

8. You meet your advisor in the hall after a concert. Greet him.

Partings

I. Dialogues

1. Dr. Marvin is Susan's advisor. They have known each other for one year, but have not had much personal contact. It's Friday afternoon, and they pass each other in the hall.

Susan:	Goodbye, Dr. Marvin.
Dr. Marvin:	Goodbye, Susan.
Susan:	Have a nice weekend.
Dr. Marvin:	Thank you, the same to you.

2. Pete and John are undergraduate students. They work in the same office together. It is Friday afternoon.

John:	Bye, Pete.
Pete:	Take it easy, John.
John:	Have a nice weekend.
Pete:	Thanks. You too.

3. Chris and Deb are taking a computer class together. Chris has been helping Deb with her homework.

Deb:	I've got to go. Thanks for your help, Chris.
Chris:	Sure, anytime.
Deb:	See you in class tomorrow. Bye.
Chris:	See you.

4. Mrs. Allen is the secretary for the English department. She has been helping Takeshi, a new student, with the registration forms.

Takeshi:	Thank you for your help, Mrs. Allen. I have to leave now.
Mrs. Allen:	You're welcome, Takeshi.
Takeshi:	Goodbye.
Mrs. Allen:	Goodbye.

II. Analysis

1. Which dialogues are more formal? Less formal?
2. Is it polite to excuse yourself from a conversation ("I've got to go") in your country? Explain.

III. Phrases

Many of these phrases can be used both formally and informally. Other factors determine how they are interpreted; for example, if a first name is used or a title and last name, and if contractions are used. These phrases are marked with an asterisk (*).

Formal

Statement	*Response*
1. Goodbye, Dr./Mr./Ms. *last name*.	Goodbye,...
2. *I hope to see you again sometime.	Yes, goodbye./Me too.
3. *Have a nice weekend.	You too.
4. Excuse me, I have to be leaving now.	Goodbye.

Informal

Statement	*Response*
1. Bye.	Bye-bye.
Take care.	
Take it easy.	You too.
2. *See you { later. / tomorrow. / in class. / at 3:00.	Yeah, bye.
3. *Have a { nice weekend. / good vacation. / great evening.	Thanks, you too.
4. I've got to go.	Bye, see you later.
*I have to go now.	

Can you add any?

IV. Practice

A. Write a response. Which ones are formal, which informal? How do you know?

1. Bob, I'd like to talk longer, but I've got to go.

2. OK, we'll meet at the student union at 7:30, then.

3. Well, Ben, I'll see you after spring vacation.

4. Dr. Chapman, I hope to see you again sometime.

B. Situations

1. You are leaving the university and may never come back. Say goodbye to the department chairman, whom you don't know very well.
2. You are talking to Andy and suddenly you remember you have an appointment in five minutes.
3. You are in a hurry. You see Daniela, your classmate. You want to talk with her but you don't have much time.
4. Professor Davis is helping you with an assignment and it is late. Tell him goodbye and thank him for his help.
5. You are at the ESL Center, asking about classes for your sister. Thank the director and leave.
6. You are at the local cultural center. They have given you information on musical concerts in the city. Thank the clerk and leave.
7. Your new neighbor just explained the newspaper delivery system to you. Thank her and say goodbye.
8. Your roommate is leaving on a trip to Niagara Falls. Say goodbye.

Introductions

I. Dialogues

1. Dave and Steve are freshmen at college. They meet after class and return to the dorm where they see Tom, Steve's roommate.

    Steve: Dave, this is Tom, my roommate.
    Dave: Hi, Tom. How's it going?
    Tom: Fine. Busy but fine.
    Steve: Well, we're off to the cafeteria.
    Tom: Nice meeting you.
    Dave: Same here. Take it easy.

2. At a business lunch, Mrs. Crean is introducing her colleague, Mr. Johnson, to Mr. Baker. Mr. Baker works for a different company and has a higher position.

    Mrs. Crean: Mr. Baker, I would like you to meet Mr. Johnson. Mr. Baker works for IBM.
    Mr. J: How do you do.
    Mr. Baker: It's a pleasure to meet you.
    Mr. J: What department are you in at IBM?

3. At the same business lunch, two men are sitting next to each other. They don't know each other, so they introduce themselves.

    Patrick: Hello, let me introduce myself. My name is Patrick Butler.
    Martin: How do you do, Mr. Butler. My name is Martin Collins.
    Patrick: Please, call me Patrick.
    Martin: Thank you, Patrick. Call me Martin.

4. Gina is introducing her niece, Annette, to her coworker, Sara, an older woman.

Gina: Sara, this is my niece, Annette. She is visiting me for a couple of
           weeks.
Sara: Hi, Annette. Nice to meet you.
Annette: Nice to meet you, too.

II. Analysis

1. For formal introductions, the woman is usually introduced to the man. (In other
   words, her name is said first: Mrs. Smith, this is . . .) In general, the older person
   is introduced to the younger person. In other cases, the person with the higher
   rank is introduced to the person with lower rank.
2. It is the custom for men to shake hands when they are introduced. If a woman
   wishes to shake hands, she should extend her hand first. The decision is hers.
3. It is polite to add some information about the person being introduced.
4. Which dialogues are more formal? Less formal?
5. Introductions are quite short in the American culture. How do you feel about the
   way Americans introduce each other? How does your culture handle
   introductions?

6. In the second dialogue Mr. Baker is introduced first. Why? Is the order of introductions important in your culture? Explain.
7. Can someone introduce him/herself in your culture? If not, explain.
8. In the third dialogue Mr. Butler and Mr. Collins quickly switch to first names. Are you comfortable doing that with someone you have just met?

III. Phrases

Formal

1. *When you meet*
   a. Dr. / Mrs. / Ms. { *last name/ first and last name,* }   I would like to introduce you to / I'd like you to meet   Dr. / Mrs. / Ms. { *last name/ first and last name.* }

   She / He } is {
   a high school science teacher.
   the chief of police.
   a civil engineer.
   a good friend of mine.

   b. Let me introduce myself.

2. *Responses*
   a. How do you do. (no answer expected)
   b. It is a pleasure to meet you.
   c. Nice to meet you.

3. *When you part*
   a. It was nice meeting you.
   b. I hope to see you again.
   c. Goodbye.

Informal

1. *When you meet*
   a. *First name,* / *First and last name,* } this is { *first name.* / *first and last name.* }
   b. Hi, my name is . . .

2. *When you part*
   a. Nice meeting you.
   b. Bye.
      Take care.
      See you.

   Can you add any?

IV. Practice

A. Write a response. Where might these people be? Are your responses formal or informal?

   1. Mr. Katz, I would like you to meet Dr. Lewis, professor of economics.

   2. Hi, my name's Nancy.

   3. Joe, this is Bill Adams, a good friend of mine.

   4. Let me introduce myself. My name is Robert Harms.

B. Situations

   1. Introduce yourself to Carol, a new girl in your class.
   2. Introduce Dongming, a good friend of yours, to Mohammed. Tell Mohammed some things about Dongming.
   3. Introduce yourself to Mr. Parson, the foreign student advisor. Ask him how to find an English class for your wife. Then tell him goodbye.
   4. Your mother is visiting for a month. Introduce her to your neighbor, Mr. Grimes.
   5. You are waiting for the bus. You see your neighbor. You don't know her, but you would like to. Introduce yourself.
   6. Your cousin, Jose, is traveling in the U.S. and comes to see you for the weekend. Introduce him to your professor.
   7. You are at a conference with Sam Tipman, a person from your office. You introduce him to Debbie Kaufman, a woman you knew at school.
   8. Introduce your brother, Dan, to your classmate. Dan is looking for a job here in this city.

Telephone Conversations

I. Dialogues

1. Jose is calling Dr. Hall, a professor in the chemistry department.

Secretary: Hello.
Jose: Hello. Is Dr. Hall there?
Secretary: Who is calling, please?
Jose: This is Jose.
Secretary: Thank you. Just a minute, please.

2. Linda is calling Carol and John's apartment. She wants to talk to John.

Carol: Hello.
Linda: Hi, Carol, this is Linda. Is John there?
Carol: Sure. Hang on.

3. Dan is calling Dr. Simon in order to make an appointment. Dr. Simon is chairman of the psychology department.

Secretary: Good morning. Dr. Simon's office.
Dan: Hello. May I speak to Dr. Simon?
Secretary: I'm sorry. He's not here now. Would you like to leave a message?
Dan: When will he be back?
Secretary: In an hour or so.
Dan: OK, I'll call him back later. Thank you.
Secretary: Mm-hmm. Goodbye.
Dan: Goodbye.

4. Fuliang and Toshi are classmates. It's Friday night.

Toshi: Hello.
Fuliang: Hi, Toshi. This is Fuliang. Do you want to go out for pizza tonight?
Toshi: I can't. I have too much work. What about tomorrow night?
Fuliang: Fine. I'll stop by at 6:00.
Toshi: Good. See you then.
Fuliang: Bye.

5. Kathy is trying to call Linda.

Scott: Hello.
Kathy: May I speak to Linda, please?
Scott: I'm sorry, you have the wrong number.
Kathy: I'm sorry. (hangs up)

Requests for Using a Telephone

1. Peter is in the library. He asks the person at the desk where to find a pay phone.

Peter: Excuse me, where is the nearest pay phone?
Librarian: Just go out that door and turn left.
Peter: Thank you.
Librarian: You're welcome.

2. Mao is in the office of the English Language and Culture Center and he needs to make a phone call.

Mao: Excuse me, is there a pay phone near here?
Secretary: Are you making a local call?
Mao: Yes.
Secretary: You can use my phone. It's on the desk.
Mao: Thank you very much.
Secretary: Sure.

Answering Machines

Answering machines are very common. When people are not home, the machine will play a prerecorded message and then record a message from the caller. Don't be afraid to use these machines. The message you will hear might sound like one of these:

You have reached the Smith home. We aren't here now, but leave a message at the sound of the beep. We'll get back to you as soon as we can.

This is 264–5900. No one is here now to answer your call. If you leave your name, number, and date and time of call at the sound of the beep, we will get back to you.

Be sure to wait until you hear the "beep," a long tone. Then, leave your information in this order:

1. Name (speak slowly and clearly)
2. Phone number
3. Date and time you called (only if they ask for it)
4. Reason you called (*briefly*—if you have time)

Here are some possible responses.

This is Inhan Kim at extension 7499. Please call me about the schedule for spring classes.

My name is George Ma, and my number is 377–4863. I would like to buy the chair you are selling.

This is Mary Polson at 267–5544. It's Monday, July 9, at 9:45 A.M. Please call me as soon as possible.

II. Analysis

1. Which dialogues are more formal? Less formal?
2. Americans almost always end telephone conversations with "goodbye" (or "bye-bye"). In what situation don't we use this closing (see dialogues)? Does your culture require such a closing?
3. Who can close a telephone call in your country? The caller or the receiver, or either of the two?
4. Do American telephone conversations seem more polite or less polite than what you would expect at home?

III. Phrases

Formal

Statement	*Response*
1. Hello	
2. Is Dr./Mr./Ms. *last name* there?	Just a minute, please.
3. May I speak to him/her?	Who is it, please?

4. I'm afraid you have the wrong number.
5. Could you repeat that, please?
6. I'm sorry, Dr./Mr./Ms. *last name*
   isn't home.
7. Can you call back later?
   Can I have him/her call you back?
8. Would you like to leave a message?

Informal

Statement   *Response*

1. Hello. (Always answer "hello" when
   you answer the telephone.)
2. Is *first name* there?   Sure. Yes.
3. Can I talk to *first name* please?   Hang on.
                                               Hold on.

Requests for using a telephone. If you are in a public place, you should always ask for the nearest pay phone. Don't ask to use a private phone.

1. Excuse me, could you tell me where the nearest pay phone is?
2. Is there a pay phone near here?

IV. Practice

A. Write a response. Are they formal or informal? Why?

1. Hello, is Dr. Kenney there?

2. Hi, Jane. Is Rose there?

3. Good morning. Linguistics Department.

4. We are sorry. We cannot answer the phone right now. Please leave your name and number at the sound of the beep.

B. Situations. The following situations require two students: student A, on this page, and student B on the next page.

Student A

1. Call your friend Louisa and ask her for a grammar assignment that you missed.
2. Call your dentist, Dr. Parker, to make an appointment.
3. Call the bus company to find out how to get to the football stadium.
4. Call the police department and report that you have been robbed.
5. Call Susan. Ed answers the phone. Ask to speak to Susan.
6. Call the public library to find out when it closes.
7. You are in the university library. Ask a librarian where the nearest pay phone is.
8. Call your landlord, Mrs. Perkins, to complain about the noisy neighbors.

Student B

1. Your friend, Pat, calls. You don't have the information she wants.
2. You are the secretary for Dr. Parker, a very busy dentist. People wanting appointments have to wait at least six weeks.
3. You work for the bus company. You don't have any information about bus routes, though. The number for that is 774-9288.
4. You take calls for the police department. Find out what the problem is and get names and addresses. Tell them a policeman is coming.
5. You are Susan's husband, Ed. Susan is at a movie tonight. Take a message.
6. You are at home. Someone calls and asks for the public library. Tell the caller that he or she has called the wrong number.
7. You work in the library. There are no pay phones in this building. The nearest one is across the street.
8. You work with Mrs. Perkins, who owns several apartment buildings. She is out to lunch right now and won't be back for an hour. Take a message.

Getting Someone's Attention

I. Dialogues

1. Ahmed is in class, and he doesn't understand what the professor just said.

Ahmed:	Excuse me, Dr. Grimes.
Dr. Grimes:	Yes?
Ahmed:	Would you repeat your last question?
Dr. Grimes:	Certainly. What are two major causes of World War II?

2. John and Wen-Yang are passing each other as they walk across campus. It's Saturday night.

Wen-Yang:	Hey, John!
John:	Hi, Wen-Yang. How's it going?
Wen-Yang:	OK. Are you going to the party tonight?
John:	I don't know. I guess so.

3. Dimitry is in a fast-food restaurant when he sees Mrs. Donio, his former English teacher. He is happy to see her and eager to talk to her. He enjoyed her classes very much and used to talk to her often after class.

Dimitry:	Mrs. Donio!
Mrs. Donio:	Oh, hello, Dimitry!
Dimitry:	I haven't seen you for so long. How are you?
Mrs. Donio:	I'm fine, just very busy. And you?

4. Two women are in a restaurant eating lunch. The waitress seems to be very busy.

First Woman:	Excuse me, Miss. Could we please have some more water?
Waitress:	Of course.

II. Analysis

1. It is often acceptable to interrupt a professor politely in American classrooms, even while she or he is lecturing. Watch what the other students do in order to know if this is all right in your situation.

2. If you go to see someone in an office, don't just walk in. If there is a secretary, tell the secretary whom you wish to see. If there is no secretary, knock on the office door and wait until you are invited to go in.

3. Which dialogues are more formal? Less formal?

4. Don't whistle to get someone's attention; it is considered impolite and most women don't like it.

5. A waitress is addressed as "Miss," a male waiter as "Waiter." Or you can just say, "Excuse me." If the waiter or waitress is a distance away, try to catch his/her eye or raise a hand slightly. Do not clap your hands or snap your fingers.

6. How do you get a waiter's or waitress's attention in your country?

7. Does it surprise you that Americans use formal and polite language with waiters and clerks and other service people? If yes, explain.

8. Americans will sometimes tap someone on the shoulder to get their attention. How would that action be interpreted in your culture?

9. "Hey, *first name*" can be insulting if used in the wrong context, or can even be perceived as a threat ("Hey, you"). Given this information, in what situations should you use it?

III. Phrases

Formal

Statement	*Situation*
1. Excuse me. Pardon me.	to a stranger
2. Excuse me, Dr./Mr./Mrs./Ms./Miss *last name.*	to a teacher inside or outside of class
3. Excuse me, could you help me? Pardon me, could I have some help?	to a clerk in a store
4. Excuse me, Miss. Excuse me. Waiter.	to a waitress in a restaurant to a waiter in a restaurant

Informal

1. *First name,* (e.g., Joe,...)
2. Hey, *first name* (e.g., Hey, Joe ...)

There are also nonverbal means of getting attention:

1. Wave of a hand
2. Tap on the shoulder (only to people you know well)
3. Raise the hand (in class, in a restaurant)
   Can you add any?

IV. Practice

A. Write a response. Is the situation formal or informal? How do you know?

   1. Excuse me. Could you help me please?

   2. Pardon me, Miss Jones.

   3. Hey, Ben!

   4. Oh, Mrs. Steen?

B. Situations

   1. You are at a restaurant and you have finished eating. You want to order dessert. Get the attention of the waitress, who is on the other side of the room, and place your order.
   2. You are at a party and you see a person you would like to meet. Get his or her attention and introduce yourself.
   3. You are at a supermarket. You are looking for canned fruit and you can't find it. Get the attention of a clerk and ask him where to find it.
   4. You are lost in a strange city. Get the attention of a stranger and ask him directions to the bus station.
   5. You promised to meet Jane in front of the bookstore. You are fifteen minutes late and when you arrive, she has left. You see her a half block away. Get her attention and apologize for being late.
   6. You are in a large department store and you want to buy some shirts. There are two clerks talking at the cash register. Get their attention and ask for help.
   7. You are in Professor Clark's economics class. You didn't understand what she just said. Get her attention and ask her to repeat what she said.
   8. You are in the post office, waiting for the clerk. She is talking to a coworker and doesn't see you. Get her attention and ask for some stamps.

Invitations

I. Dialogues

1. Jean and Maria, two students, are talking in the hall. They have just finished their associate's degrees in computer science. Even though they were in the same program, they don't know each other very well.

> Jean: I'd like to invite you to a graduation reception. It's at my house at 8:30 Friday evening. Can you come?
>
> Maria: I'd be glad to come, but I will be a little late.
>
> Jean: That's all right. Just come when you can.
>
> Maria: Thank you. It's very nice of you to invite me.

2. Jean and Sally are chatting on the bus on their way to work. They are both summer interns at a law office.

> Sally: Jean, can you come to a party at my place Friday evening?
>
> Jean: Thanks, I'd love to. What time?
>
> Sally: About 8:00.

Jean: What should I bring?
Sally: Oh, just bring some chips.
Jean: OK, see you then.

3. Dan and Jay are friends who live in the same apartment building. They often try to get together on the weekends.

Dan: How about going to dinner tomorrow night at the Steak House?
Jay: I can't. I'm going to D.C. for the weekend.
Dan: What about next Friday instead?
Jay: Great. I'll plan on it.
Dan: Is 6:00 all right with you?
Jay: Fine.

4. Mei and Janice are roommates. Janice's parents are visiting from out of town and Janice invites Mei to go out with them.

Janice: Would you like to join us tomorrow night? We're going to go to the Steak House.
Mei: I'd love to, but I can't. I'm going to New York for the weekend.
Janice: Oh, I'm sorry, We'll make it another time.
Mei: Thank you very much for the invitation anyway.

II. Analysis

1. "I'd love to" is a phrase most often used by women and girls. Men typically don't use it.
2. "Can I take a raincheck?" means that you must refuse the invitation but that you want the person to offer the same invitation again soon.
3. In informal invitations, the person who does the inviting (to a movie, coffee, dinner, etc.) is not necessarily expected to pay for everything. If the invitation is stated: "Let's go out for coffee" or "How about going out to lunch Thursday," usually both people pay separately. But if the invitation is stated, "Let me take/ treat you to lunch/a movie/etc.," then the inviter expects to pay. Also, if a man invites a woman, as a date, the man is usually expected to pay.
4. In informal situations, especially among students or other young people who are on a limited income, it is common for the host or hostess to ask if you can bring something to a party. People often combine their resources in order to have more food and drinks at a party.

5. Americans often say, "Let's get together sometime" or "I'll give you a call sometime" without being specific about when and where. This is really a way of saying "I enjoyed meeting you" and is not the same as a definite invitation. Don't expect the person to always call you or follow up with a definite invitation. These indefinite statements may simply mean "I enjoyed spending this time together."

6. Which dialogues are formal? Informal?

7. When Americans cannot accept an invitation, they usually turn it down (say no), and no one's feelings are hurt provided a reasonable excuse is given. How would this practice be received in your country?

8. If an American invites you to dinner, you are expected to arrive on time. For most parties, however, you may arrive late. How is this different from your culture?

III. Phrases

Formal

1. *The invitation*
   a. I would like to invite you to . . .
   b. Would you like to . . .

2. *Accepting the invitation*
   a. Thank you. $\begin{cases} \text{I'd be glad to come} \\ \text{I'd like to very much.} \end{cases}$
   b. It's nice of you to invite me.

3. *Refusing the invitation*
   a. I'm very sorry, but . . .
   b. I would like very much to go, but . . .
   c. It's very kind of you to invite me, but . . .
   d. I hope you'll invite me again sometime.
   e. Can I take a raincheck?

Informal

1. *The invitation*
   a. Can you come to . . . ?
   b. How about going to . . . ?

2. *Accepting the invitation*

Thanks. $\begin{cases} \text{I'd love to.} \\ \text{I'd like to.} \\ \text{That would be nice.} \end{cases}$

3. *Refusing the invitation:*
   a. Thanks, but . . .
   b. I'm sorry, but . . .
   c. I'd love to, but . . .
   d. Maybe some other time?

   Can you add any to these?

IV. Practice

A. Write an invitation and a response. Should the invitation be formal or informal? Why?

   1. Martha is a woman who lives in the apartment across from Betsy's. She seems very nice, but Betsy hasn't had a chance to get to know her yet. Martha asks Betsy if she would like to spend Sunday afternoon at her parents' house with her.
   2. Two of Alfredo's coworkers are going to a baseball game on Saturday. They invite Alfredo to go along. He is busy, but he really wishes he could go.
   3. Ahmed invites his friend, Salim, for coffee after class.
   4. Savine's neighbor invites her to drive out to a local park for the afternoon with her family. Savine has too much work to go.

B. Situations

   1. Invite your classmate to dinner. Be sure to include time and date.
   2. Ricardo asks you to go to a movie tomorrow night. Refuse politely.
   3. You are a department chairperson. Invite your student to attend a lecture. Be sure to include time and date.
   4. Invite your office mate home for a special traditional meal next Friday night.
   5. Invite your advisor to come over and meet your family one evening next week.
   6. You meet your good friend, Ann. Invite her to go to a concert with you next weekend.
   7. See if your office mate wants to go out for pizza after you finish work.
   8. Invite your neighbor whom you know very well over for coffee after dinner.

Requesting Clarification

I. Dialogues

1. Michael and Rachel meet Peter, a new friend of Michael's. Michael introduces them.

Michael:	Rachel, I'd like you to meet a friend of mine, Peter Brandenburg.
Rachel:	Sorry, I didn't get your last name?
Peter:	Brandenburg.
Rachel:	Oh, Brandenburg. Nice to meet you.

2. Mr. Ginsberg is finishing up his grammar class on Friday afternoon.

Mr. G:	Class, put away your books now. Get out a piece of paper and a pen.
Michael:	Excuse me, Mr. Ginsberg, what did you say?
Mr. G:	I said that you need some paper and a pen.
Michael:	Oh, is this a quiz?
Mr. G:	Yes, it is!

3. Lori is out shopping for a new dress. She is speaking with the salesclerk.

Lori:	I'd like to pay by check if that is all right.
Clerk:	Do you have identification?
Lori:	Pardon me?
Clerk:	Do you have any identification with you?
Lori:	Oh yes. Is my driver's license OK?
Clerk:	Thank you.

4. Ahmed and Jack are walking back to their dorm. Ahmed is daydreaming.

Jack:	Ahmed, have you studied for your sociology test yet?
Ahmed:	Huh? What did you say?
Jack:	Have you studied for sociology yet?
Ahmed:	No. I haven't even finished the reading yet!

II. Analysis

1. Which dialogues are more formal? Less formal?
2. Is it acceptable in your culture to ask for clarification in the situations presented in these dialogues?
3. Do you think there might be situations in the U.S. when it would not be appropriate to request clarification? If so, when?

III. Phrases

Formal

1. I beg your pardon?
   Pardon me?
   Excuse me?
2. Excuse me, what did you say?
3. I'm sorry. I don't understand you.
4. Would you mind repeating what you said?

Informal

1. What?
   Huh?
2. (I'm sorry) what did you say?
3. What was that again?

   Can you add any to these?

IV. Practice

A. Complete the dialogues.

1. Chien is introducing Mr. Porta, her supervisor, to Nancy Anderson, Chien's cousin.

   Chien: Mr. Porta, I'd like you to meet Nancy Anderson, my cousin.

   Mr. Porta: I'm sorry, I didn't get your last name.

   Nancy:

   Mr. Porta:

2. Ayuko doesn't understand the next question on an oral exam.

   Teacher: Question number two is, "Why was the soldier so sad?"

   Ayuko: Excuse me?

   Teacher:

   Ayuko:

3. Janet asks her classmate, Karen, a question, but Janet doesn't hear her answer.

   Janet: Karen, what are you doing after class today?

   Karen:

   Janet:

   Karen:

4. Pierre is in a bookstore. He asks the price of a calendar, but he doesn't understand the clerk's answer.

   Pierre: How much is this calendar, please?

   Clerk:

   Pierre:

   Clerk:

B. Situations

1. Tell Luis your phone number. He is trying to write it down, and doesn't remember it.
2. Ask Christa what time it is. She doesn't understand your question.
3. Introduce yourself to one of your classmates. He/she doesn't hear your last name.
4. Sandy is a clerk in a record store. Jose is a customer who asks for a specific record album. Sandy doesn't hear what Jose says.
5. Martin is a clerk in the post office. He tells you the price of an airmail letter to Japan. You don't understand.
6. Joseph invites Dominica to an informal party at his house. Dominica accepts but doesn't hear the time.
7. Sarah is a saleswoman in a store. Maria asks where the restrooms are but doesn't hear the answer.
8. Barbara works in the library. Chom asks when the library closes but doesn't understand the answer.

Eating at a Restaurant

I. Dialogues

1. Kathy and a friend are out for lunch at a popular restaurant. They have been talking and so they are not ready to order their food.

Waitress:	May I take your order?
Kathy:	We're not quite ready yet.
Waitress:	OK, I'll come back in a few minutes.
Kathy:	Thank you.

2. Ken is eating dinner at a local steak house. He is ready to order now.

Waiter:	May I take your order now?
Ken:	Yes, I'd like the steak dinner.
Waiter:	How would you like your meat?
Ken:	Medium.
Waiter:	Mashed or baked potatoes?
Ken:	Mashed.
Waiter:	Green beans or summer squash?
Ken:	I'll take the green beans.
Waiter:	Tossed salad or cole slaw?
Ken:	The tossed salad with Italian dressing.
Waiter:	Anything to drink?
Ken:	Yes. Coffee, please.

3. Ron and a friend are eating dinner at an elegant restaurant. They were served their food a few minutes ago. The waitress comes back to speak to them.

Waitress:	Is everything all right here?
Ron:	Yes, thank you. Everything is delicious. Oh, could I have some more water, please?
Waitress:	Yes, of course.
Ron:	Thank you.

4. Janet has just finished lunch at a sandwich shop. She needs to leave soon to get back to work.

Waitress:	Will there be anything else? Dessert?
Janet:	No, thank you. Could I have the check, please?
Waitress:	Sure.

II. Analysis

1. Americans are polite and formal with waiters and waitresses. How are they treated in your culture?
2. "Separate checks" means that each person will get a check and pay separately. Be sure to ask for this *before* you give the waitress your order.
3. In the U.S., a waiter or waitress receives a tip, usually about 15 percent of the total bill (it is not included in your bill). Most people leave the tip on the table. Waiters and waitresses receive very low wages and depend on the tips as part of their income. What is the tipping custom in your culture?
4. If something is wrong with the food (for example, too cold, too salty, not fresh), Americans often tell the waiter, who usually corrects the problem. Would you do this in your country? If not, why? Do you think you would feel comfortable doing it here?
5. Usually, each person at a table orders his or her own food. What is the custom in your culture?

III. Phrases

Ordering at a restaurant is usually formal because you don't know the waitress or waiter.

1. *Waitress/waiter*
   a. May I help you?
   b. Would you like a drink before dinner?
   c. May I take your order?
   d. How would you like your meat? (answer: rare, medium, or well-done)
   e. Baked potato, french fries, or rice pilaf?
   f. Corn, beets, or green beans?
   g. Salad dressing? (answer: tell what kind of dressing you want)
   h. Anything to drink?

i. Is everything all right here?

j. Will there be anything else?

2. *Fast-food restaurants*. Clerks in fast-food restaurants are always in a hurry, so they speak in short or abbreviated sentences.

a. May I help you?

b. Drinks?

c. Fries with that?

d. Anything else?

e. For here or to go? (Are you going to eat here, or do you want to take the food with you?)

3. *Customer*

a. We haven't decided yet.

b. We're ready to order now.

c. What comes with the dinner?

d. Could we have separate checks, please?

e. Excuse me, could I please have some more . . . ?

f. Is tea/coffee/dessert included with the dinner?

g. May I have the check please?

Can you add any?

IV. Practice

A. Write dialogues between a customer and a waitress.

1. You are in a small café. You just want to order some coffee and dessert.

2. You and three other friends are in a crowded sandwich shop for lunch. Place your order, first being sure to ask for separate checks.

3. You have just started your meal at an expensive French restaurant and you discover that there is no salt on your table. Ask the waiter for some when he checks to see that everything is OK.

4. You have just finished eating your breakfast. When the waitress offers you more coffee, ask for the check.

B. Situations. Pretend you are in a restaurant, and order lunch or dinner from the following menu. Your instructor will act as a waiter/waitress unless you are familiar with the situation and can act out this part yourself.

DINNERS

Baked Meat Loaf with Brown Gravy $5.95
Baby Beef Liver and Onions $6.95
Grilled Pork Chop with Apple Sauce $10.95
Veal Parmigiana $11.95
Broiled Ham Steak with Pineapple Ring $8.95
Broiled Haddock $10.95
Fried Shrimp $12.95
Baked Scrod $11.95
Fried Chicken (3 pieces) $8.95
Grilled Sirloin Steak $11.95
Grilled Fillet Mignon Steak with Mushrooms $14.95

The above dinners include a choice of potato and vegetable or salad.

Salads: Tossed Salad or Cole Slaw
Dressings: French, Italian, Ranch or Thousand Island
Vegetables: Green Beans, Corn, Zucchini, Peas
Potatoes: French Fried, Baked, Mashed, Rice Pilaf

Beverages:

Coffee (regular or decaffeinated) 65
Tea 65
Milk . . . . .75 & .85
Soft Drinks . . . . .65, .75 & .85

Sandwiches

Platter includes choice of two: French fries, coleslaw, tossed salad, or soup.

	platter	a la carte
Hamburger	$4.95	$3.95
Cheeseburger	$5.15	$4.15
Ham and Cheese Club	$5.95	$4.95
Grilled Cheese	$3.95	$2.95
Grilled Reuben (corned beef, cheese and sauerkraut)	$5.95	$4.95
Fried Fish	$4.95	$3.95
Bacon, Lettuce 'n Tomato	$3.95	$2.95
Chicken Sandwich	$4.95	$3.95
Hot Roast Beef with potatoes and gravy	$6.95	$5.95

Soups: cup $1.25   bowl $1.75

Salads:

Tossed Salad $1.25
Cottage Cheese and Fruit $1.25
Fresh Fruit $1.95
Cole Slaw $1.25
Chef's Salad $4.95
   with turkey, ham, hard-boiled egg, cheese and fresh greens

Excuses and Apologies

I. Dialogues

1. Louisa was late for her morning class. Class is over now, and she apologizes to the instructor, Dr. Carlson.

Dr. Carlson:	Oh, hello Louisa.
Louisa:	Good morning, Dr. Carlson. Please excuse me for being late today. I overslept.
Dr. Carlson:	Certainly. We'll see you tomorrow at 9:00, then.

2. John and Keith are talking on John's front porch. Yesterday they had an argument over where Keith had parked his car, and today Keith wants to apologize.

Keith:	Hey, John, I'm sorry about what happened yesterday.
John:	That's OK. It was my fault.
Keith:	No, I was just in a bad mood, that's all.
John:	Well, let's forget about it.

3. Joan and Tom were supposed to meet at the bus stop at 7:00 to go to a play. Joan is ten minutes late.

Joan:	I'm glad you're still here! Sorry I'm so late.
Tom:	Don't worry. The bus hasn't come yet.
Joan:	I was just walking out the door when the phone rang. It was my mother, and you know how she talks!
Tom:	I'm surprised you weren't later!

4. Elizabeth is talking to her sociology professor, Mrs. Larson. During a class discussion yesterday on gun control, she became very angry and shouted at another student.

Elizabeth:	Mrs. Larson?
Mrs. Larson:	Yes?
Elizabeth:	Please excuse me for losing my temper in class yesterday.
Mrs. Larson:	That's quite all right. Was something troubling you?
Elizabeth:	Yes. A friend of mine was nearly killed by a handgun. I guess I was more upset than I thought.

5. Maria and Jenny are two friends who meet after a two-week spring break.

Jenny: How was your vacation, Maria?
Maria: I had such a good time. I hated to come back.
Jenny: Did you get my postcard?
Maria: Yes, thanks. I'm sorry I didn't write to you, too—I meant to, but I was just so busy with my family!
Jenny: That's OK. I knew you wouldn't have much time.

II. Analysis

1. If you are late to a class, *take your seat quietly* without saying anything. In the U.S., it is rude to interrupt the class to apologize when you first enter. Wait until after the class to speak to the instructor (see dialogue 1).
2. Ask your instructor to discuss with you the different kinds of situations that require apologies or excuses, for example, being late or forgetting to write, which require only a single statement as opposed to more serious situations (losing your temper or hurting someone's feelings), which require a more extensive apology.
3. Apologies are most often accompanied by an explanation of how the situation happened.
4. Which dialogues are more formal? Less formal?
5. In your country, would you apologize in all of these situations? Would your apologies be short or long? Are apologies ever not accepted? If so, under what circumstances?
6. Do you think Americans apologize too much? Not enough?
7. Do you feel Americans are sincere when they make (and accept) apologies?
8. Is it important to apologize for being late to an appointment, a dinner, or a party in your culture?

III. Phrases

Formal

Excuse/Apology   *Response*

1. Excuse me, please.
   Pardon me.
   I'm very sorry. $\begin{cases} \text{Of course.} \\ \text{Certainly.} \end{cases}$
   I'm sorry.
   I beg your pardon.
2. Excuse me for being late.
   I'm sorry I'm late.   That's quite all right.
   Excuse me for a moment, please.

   I'm sorry I forgot to $\begin{cases} \text{call.} \\ \text{come.} \\ \text{inform you.} \\ \text{answer your} \\ \text{\ \ letter.} \end{cases}$ Think nothing of it.
   I'm sorry I didn't

   I'm sorry, but I must leave early.
3. I apologize.
   I apologize for losing my temper. $\begin{cases} \text{That's quite all right.} \\ \text{Think nothing of it.} \\ \text{Don't worry about it.} \end{cases}$
   Please excuse my behavior yesterday.
   I'm sorry. I didn't mean to hurt your
      feelings.

Informal

Excuse/Apology   *Response*

1. Excuse me.   It's OK.
   I'm sorry.   Don't worry.
   Sorry.   Sure.
2. Sorry I'm late.   It's all right.

   Sorry I forgot to $\begin{cases} \text{call.} \\ \text{write.} \\ \text{come.} \\ \text{tell you.} \end{cases}$

3. Just a minute. I'll be right back.
   Sorry about yesterday.
   I'm sorry about yesterday.

The informal responses can be used for any apology.
Can you add any?

IV. Practice

A. Write dialogues for these situations. Are they formal or informal? Why?

1. Toshi and Sam meet in the hallway of their department after summer vacation. They are both graduate students in the computer science department, and they know each other fairly well. Sam sent Toshi several postcards but didn't receive any in return. Toshi apologizes for this.
2. Carlos is late for Mrs. Wilson's class again. He has been late the last three days because his car is not running properly. He apologizes after class.
3. Mindy and Nancy made plans to meet at a party last night, but Mindy forgot to call Nancy to tell her where it was. She apologizes the next day.
4. Randy asks Dr. Lewis, his chemistry professor, if he can turn in his lab report late. He apologizes for the inconvenience to Dr. Lewis.

B. Situations

1. You are in class, and suddenly you don't feel very well.
2. Apologize to your brother for yelling at him because he lost several of your tapes.
3. You are at a friend's house for dinner. You have to leave early to study for a test the next day.
4. You had an appointment with your advisor, Professor Johnson, at 10:30. You didn't get there until 10:50.
5. Your neighbor asks you to help him move a couch. You have to say no because you have a bad back. Apologize and explain.
6. You told Fred you would come over to study with him last night and you forgot. He sees you and asks why you didn't come.
7. You borrowed a book from your neighbor and promised to return it the next day, but you forgot it at work. Apologize and explain.
8. You borrowed a pen from a classmate and then lost it. Apologize.

Hiding Feelings

I. Dialogues

1. Lynn and Jessie are new roommates who don't yet know each other very well. Lynn is showing Jessie a new dress.

   Lynn: How do you like my new dress?
   Jesse: Oh, it's very unusual.
   Lynn: Shall I wear it to the party, or shall I wear the blue and white one?
   Jesse: They are both nice, but I think I prefer the blue and white dress.

2. Will and Steve are discussing a department party they attended last night.

   Will: That was quite a party.
   Steve: It sure was. Will, did you have a chance to meet Bob Jameson?
   Will: Just for a few minutes.
   Steve: What did you think of him?
   Will: He seems quite intelligent, but I really only just met him.

3. Rich is visiting Dan in the hospital. Dan had his appendix taken out.

   Rich: So, Dan, how are you? You look tired.
   Dan: OK, I guess. I'm pretty sore, but it could be worse.
   Rich: Well, I hope you're getting lots of rest.
   Dan: Thanks. I'm sure I'll feel better tomorrow.

II. Analysis

1. What might Jessie's true feelings be about Lynn's new dress? How and why is she hiding them?
2. What might Will's true feelings be about Bob Jameson? Why and how is he hiding them? What words does he use?
3. How might Dan really be feeling now? How and why does he hide his true feelings? What words does he use?
4. Would you hide your feelings in these situations in your own culture?
5. Can you think of some other situations in addition to those listed above when you would hide your feelings?
6. Americans think that a smile means someone is happy. Does a smile sometimes hide other feelings in your culture?
7. Americans are often very direct. If they can't come to a party or cannot help you, they will simply say no. Many other cultures hide a no by saying yes. Do you hide saying no in your culture? If so, how? Why?
8. If you comment on something different about a person (haircut, clothing, etc.), be sure to say something positive or at least neutral in addition to noticing the change.

III. Phrases

Note: The following phrases are used in several different ways. Many of them are appropriate in both formal and informal situations. Ask your instructor for further explanation.

1. *To avoid hurting someone's feelings*

    a. The { cake / dinner / soup / dessert } is very good, but I'm { full, / not very hungry, } thank you.

    b. Your new { dress / coat / hat / house } is very { interesting. / unusual. / nice. }

c. It's nice, but I think I prefer . . .

d. Bob seems $\begin{cases} \text{nice,} \\ \text{like an interesting person,} \\ \text{quite intelligent,} \end{cases}$ but I don't know him very well yet.

2. *To avoid sounding like a complainer*

a. I'm feeling all right.
I can't complain.
I could be worse.
I *have* felt better.[1]
I'm sure I'll feel better tomorrow.

3. *To avoid an argument or to politely introduce an argument*

a. I can see your point.
I guess you're right.
I agree, but . . .

Can you add any to these?

IV. Practice

A. Write dialogues for these situations. Are they formal or informal? Why?

1. You run into an acquaintance in a discount shoe store. She shows you the pair of shoes she is thinking of buying and asks your opinion. You think they are big and clumsy-looking, but you want to be polite when you answer.
2. Your neighbor's thirteen-year-old son has put a bright pink streak in his hair. He asks you what you think of it.
3. You are depressed because your car isn't running and your wallet was stolen yesterday. When your neighbor asks you how you are, you want to tell the truth, but you don't want to complain too much.
4. The stranger on the bus next to you is talking to you about the political situation in your country. He clearly doesn't know what he is talking about. You want to be polite, and you definitely want to avoid an argument.

---

1. "I *have* felt better" takes special stress on the helping verb *have* in order to express the idea that you don't really feel well now.

B. Situations

1. You are invited to an American home for dinner. You don't like the salad but you eat it. They offer you some more.

2. Your new friend is wearing a horrible shirt. He just bought it and asks you how you like it.

3. Your mother tells you that you don't look well. She asks you how you feel. You feel terrible, but you want to go to the ballgame and don't want her to know.

4. Your roommate, Wendy, is getting married to a man you really can't stand, even for a few minutes. She asks you to go to dinner with them to celebrate.

5. Your aunt has invited you over for cake on your birthday. You eat one piece, and it is really too sugary for you. She wants to serve you another piece, and you don't want to hurt her feelings, but you don't want any more.

6. Your coworker introduces you to a new friend, Elliot, at a party. Elliot seems rather noisy and unpleasant to you. Later, your coworker asks you what you think of him.

7. A local family takes you up to their favorite place to see the view of the city. You find the view unimpressive compared to sights in your country. You want to be polite to this family, though.

8. Your former coworker brings in her new baby to show off. She clearly thinks he is the most beautiful creature on earth. You think he looks a lot like E.T., but you don't want to offend her.

Compliments and Congratulations

I. Dialogues

1. Jan and Beth live in the same apartment complex. They meet in the parking lot one morning.

    Beth: Hi, Jan. How's your new job?
    Jan: Fine. I'm sort of nervous, though.
    Beth: By the way, you look really nice today.
    Jan: Thanks. I have to dress up a lot more for this job.

2. Stan and Tim are new employees in a computer firm. They knew each other in college also.

    Tom: Stan, I hear you bought a house. Congratulations!
    Stan: Thanks. I'll be paying for it for a long time, but it's worth it.
    Tom: Is it one bedroom or two?
    Stan: One. Hey, come see for yourself! The address is 252 Cedar Drive.
    Tom: Thanks. I'll take you up on that.

3. Carlos and Dr. Rosen are just leaving a departmental seminar where Carlos has given an hour-long presentation.

    Dr. Rosen: Carlos, may I see you for a moment?
    Carlos: Sure, Dr. Rosen.
    Dr. Rosen: Your presentation was quite impressive today. You seemed to know the topic thoroughly.
    Carlos: Thank you, sir. I have done a lot of research on it.
    Dr. Rosen: That was clear. Keep up the good work.

4. Your roommate's parents, Mr. and Mrs. Barnes, have invited you for Sunday dinner. They are friendly and easy to talk to.

    Mrs. Barnes: How about a piece of cake now?
    You: Thank you, yes. Everything has been so delicious!
    Mrs. Barnes: Thank you.
    You: The soup was especially good. Would you mind giving me the recipe?
    Mrs. Barnes: Of course not. I'd be happy to. I'm glad you liked it.

5. You and your spouse have been at a great party. Now it is midnight, and you have to leave. You are talking with your hostess.

> You: Well, we'd better be going. I have to work tomorrow.
> Hostess: Sorry you have to leave. Thank you for coming.
> You: Thank you! The party was great. I haven't had so much fun in a long time.
> Hostess: I'm glad you enjoyed it. See you around!

II. Analysis

1. Statements such as "I hope you enjoyed the party" are known as "fishing" (or asking) for a compliment. You should always respond with an appropriate compliment. Otherwise, you will hurt the person's feelings and maybe insult them as well.
2. Which dialogues are more formal? Less formal?
3. In theory, the American custom is to say "thank you" when someone compliments you, but many people find that accepting a compliment is difficult, and they may feel quite uncomfortable (ask your instructor for examples). This does not mean that they don't like your compliment, but that they are embarrassed by it.
4. How do you acknowledge a compliment in your culture?
5. Are there things you should not give compliments about in your culture?

III. Phrases

Formal

1. You look very $\left\{ \begin{array}{l} \text{nice} \\ \text{handsome} \\ \text{pretty} \end{array} \right\}$ today.

2. Your apartment is $\left\{ \begin{array}{l} \text{lovely.} \\ \text{beautiful.} \\ \text{very nice.} \end{array} \right.$

3. Your $\left\{ \begin{array}{l} \text{speech} \\ \text{presentation} \\ \text{class} \\ \text{lecture} \end{array} \right\}$ was $\left\{ \begin{array}{l} \text{well done.} \\ \text{excellent.} \\ \text{good.} \\ \text{impressive.} \end{array} \right.$

4. The dinner
   The dessert
   The salad   } was { delicious.
   Everything   very good.
                         very nice.

5. Your { party } was { very nice.
          reception }   very enjoyable.

6. Congratulations on { your new job.
                        your new baby.
                        your promotion.
                        your marriage.
                        your new car.

7. Congratulations!

Informal

1. You look really { good
                     great } today.
                     nice

2. What a { beautiful } { apartment.
            nice }   house.

3. Great
   Good
   Nice   } { presentation.
   Well done!   speech.

4. Good dinner!

5. The { dinner
         dessert
         food   } { was } { delicious.
         salad }   is }   very good.

6. Nice
   Great } party!

   The { party } was { great.
         picnic }   nice.

7. Congratulations!
   Congratulations on ... !

Responses. "Thank you" is an appropriate response for all of the phrases. "Thanks" is fine for informal situations. "I'm glad you enjoyed/liked it" is also acceptable.

Can you add any to these?

IV. Practice

A. Write dialogues for these situations. Are they formal or informal? Why?

1. You run into Chuck, a friend from management school. You are both looking for summer jobs in business, to get experience for your degree. When you ask him if he has found a job yet, he answers yes.
2. You meet a former classmate at a big department store at the mall. She tells you that she is going to be married next month. Congratulate her.
3. Dr. Walters, a distinguished anthropology professor, has just given a very interesting lecture in a department seminar. His topic is one that you would like to do your thesis on. Compliment him on his lecture and express your interest in the topic.
4. Your neighbor, Kim Smith, has just bought a new sports car. Compliment her on it.

B. Situations

1. Compliment your classmate on his new suit.
2. You meet one of your former teachers at a local ice cream store. She tells you that she is going to have a baby.
3. Your roommate, Sandra, is all dressed up for a very important job interview. Compliment her on her appearance.
4. You are invited out to see the new house of a good friend. You think it is beautiful.
5. You are finishing dinner at Mrs. Evans's house. She serves a chocolate cake that is wonderful.
6. You are leaving a potluck dinner (a dinner where everyone brings a dish to share). Compliment the host and hostess.
7. Your brother calls you with the good news that he has a new job.
8. You are leaving a reception for a new faculty member in your department. The food was delicious. Compliment Ms. Thompson, the secretary who organized everything.

Complaints

I. Dialogues

1. Joe and Jack are friends who play soccer together every Friday night. They are talking while they walk to the gym.

   Jack: So, Joe, how are classes?
   Joe: Oh, all right I guess, except for sociology.
   Jack: Who teaches it?
   Joe: Dr. Anderson. He's really a poor teacher.
   Jack: Too bad. I'll have to avoid that course.

2. Terry and a friend are eating out at a family restaurant. When the check comes, they discover a problem.

   Terry: Excuse me, but I think you've overcharged us.
   Waitress: Well, let's take a look.
   Terry: We had two chicken dinners, not two steak dinners.
   Waitress: Oh, I'm terribly sorry, sir. Let's see—that will be $14.95 and not $27.95.

3. Li and Betty are chemistry lab partners who get along together quite well. They are chatting while they set up their experiment.

   Li: How's it going, Betty?
   Betty: Horrible! I feel awful!
   Li: What's wrong?
   Betty: I have such a bad headache! And my eyes hurt.
   Li: It's probably the weather.
   Betty: Yes, this humidity is terrible.
   Li: And so is the pollution!

4. Jenny bought a dress yesterday and then discovered a hole in it when she got home. She takes it back to the store.

> Clerk: May I help you?
>
> Jenny: Yes. I bought this new dress here yesterday and I would like to return it.
>
> Clerk: What's the matter with it?
>
> Jenny: There is a hole in the material under the arm.
>
> Clerk: Yes, you're right. Would you like to exchange it?
>
> Jenny: I think I prefer to have my money back.

II. Analysis

1. Which dialogues are more formal? Less formal?
2. When Americans complain about a service or about merchandise, they are usually polite—unless they don't receive any help.
3. Many foreigners think Americans are too direct, and complaining is certainly a form of directness. Do you feel Americans are too direct, blunt, even rude? Would you complain about the same things as the Americans in the preceding dialogues did?
4. The third dialogue, which sometimes does occur among friends, is a bit unusual. When someone asks you how you are, he or she expects you to say you are fine or OK. It is more acceptable, however, to complain about physical ailments than about emotional problems. Does this idea bother you? Do you have a similar greeting ritual where a particular answer is expected?

III. Phrases

Formal

1. I bought this $\begin{Bmatrix} \text{dress} \\ \text{electric mixer} \\ \text{lamp} \\ \text{shirt} \end{Bmatrix}$ and I would like to $\begin{Bmatrix} \text{return it} \\ \text{exchange it.} \\ \text{have my money} \\ \text{back.} \end{Bmatrix}$

2. It doesn't work well.
   It doesn't fit.
   It's torn.
   It's dirty.

3. May I see the manager, please?

4. (I'm sorry but) I think you overcharged me.

5. There must be some mistake.

6. I think you gave me the wrong bill.

Note: These types of complaints are almost always formal.

Informal

1. The food's $\begin{cases} \text{always the same.} \\ \text{horrible.} \\ \text{terrible.} \end{cases}$

2. I hate rain.

   What awful weather.

   Is the weather $\begin{cases} \text{usually} \\ \text{always} \end{cases}$ this bad?

3. I have too much work to do.

4. I feel rotten.

   I feel so sick.

   I feel horrible.

   I have such a stomachache.

5. My $\begin{cases} \text{feet} \\ \text{head} \\ \text{stomach} \end{cases}$ hurt(s).

6. I can't believe she gave me a *C* on that test!

7. He's such a $\begin{cases} \text{bad} \\ \text{boring} \\ \text{poor} \\ \text{hard} \end{cases}$ teacher.

Can you add any?

IV. Practice

A. Write dialogues for these situations. Are they formal or informal? Why?

1. You bought a pair of shoes and when you got home you noticed that the sole was loose on one. Take them back to the store to return them.
2. Talk with Mike, a classmate, about the results of your biology exam. Mike complains about his grade and about the professor.
3. You get a phone bill which shows a $20.19 charge for a call to Venezuela. You never made this call. Call the phone company to complain.
4. Complain to your neighbor about the weather.

B. Situations

1. You went to McDonald's for a hamburger and a coke. You were charged for a milkshake you didn't order.
2. Your grammar teacher gave a test that was unreasonably long. Complain to your classmate about it. Then complain to the teacher.
3. You just bought a new pair of sandals at Wally's Shoe Store and today one of the straps broke.
4. You just received your electricity bill for the month and you are certain it is too high. Call the company and inquire about the bill.
5. You meet a friend in the student cafeteria and the food is bad, as usual.
6. You try to return a jacket that has a broken zipper. When the clerk isn't helpful, ask to see the manager.
7. It has been raining for three days. When you see Juanita, a colleague, begin a conversation by complaining about the weather.
8. When you get your check in a restaurant, you notice that you were charged for a dessert that you didn't order.

Asking and Giving Directions

I. Dialogues

1. A: Excuse me, can you tell me the way to Second Street?
    B: Sure. Go straight ahead for three blocks. Turn right at the stop sign. That's Second.
    A: Thank you very much.
    B: It's nothing.

2. A: Pardon me, can you tell me if this is the right way to Frick Park?
    B: I'm sorry; I have no idea.
    A: Thank you anyway.

3. A: Excuse me, can you tell me where Mercy Hospital is?
    B: It's downtown. Take a 71A bus and get off at Smith Road. Walk up the hill and you'll run right into it.
    A: Thanks.

II. Analysis

1. Asking and giving directions is usually formal because you are talking with strangers.
2. If someone asks you, "Is this the way to ...," just saying yes or no is not enough. You should confirm the directions, for example, "Yes it is. Just keep going straight another few blocks. It will be on your right."

III. Phrases

1. *Questions*

   a. Excuse me, can you tell me
   {
   how far it is to
   how to get to
   the way to
   if this is the right way to
   which bus goes to
   the best way to
   }
   First Avenue?

2. *Responses*
   a. Go straight ahead.
   b. Turn left.
      Take a left.
   c. It's on the { righthand side.
                    lefthand side.
   d. It'll be on your right.
   e. It's about { three blocks.
                   a mile.
                   four stop lights.
   f. You can't miss it.
   g. You'll run right into it.

   Can you add any?

IV. Practice

A. Using the following map, write a response.

1. Excuse me, can you tell me how to get to the park?

2. Pardon me, where is the Regent Theater?

3. Excuse me, is this the way to the library?

4. Excuse me, can you tell me how far it is to Blick's Department Store?

B. Situations

1. Using the map, ask and give directions to
   a. the grocery store.
   b. the post office.
   c. the bus station.
   d. the stadium.
   e. the library.
   f. the drugstore.
   g. the laundromat.
   h. the park.

2. Using knowledge of the community around you, ask and give directions from the classroom to
   a. the public library.
   b. the nearest grocery store.
   c. the nearest drugstore.
   d. the Foreign Student Office.
   e. the nearest post office.
   f. your home.
   g. the bus stop to get downtown.

Closing a Conversation

I. Dialogues

1. Brian is talking to the receptionist at your doctor's office. She is trying to explain some complicated insurance forms.

Brian:	I still don't understand what you mean. Could you explain it again?
Receptionist:	I'd like to talk about this some more, but I don't have time now. Could you come back this afternoon?
Brian:	Sure. What time?
Receptionist:	Is 3:00 all right?
Brian:	Yes.
Receptionist:	Good. See you this afternoon then.
Brian:	Goodbye.

2. Victor has been talking with the registration secretary at the English Language Center. He wants to find an evening class for his wife.

Victor:	Are you sure there are no English classes offered in the evening?
Secretary:	Yes, I am. Our last evening class ended last week.
Victor:	OK. Well, thank you for your help.
Secretary:	You're welcome.
Victor:	Goodbye.
Secretary:	Goodbye.

3. Ed and Helen are talking on the phone. Helen was away interviewing for jobs in New York last week.

Ed:	So, your trip to New York was really fun?
Helen:	Yeah. I'll tell you more about it when I see you. I've got to hang up now. My roommate is waiting to use the phone.
Ed:	OK. Maybe I'll see you at lunch.
Helen:	Fine. See you then.
Ed:	Bye.

4. Irene and Betsy run into each other in the library. They spend a few minutes chatting about Betsy's brother's engagement.

Irene: That's really good news about your brother getting married.

Betsy: We're all happy for him. Well, I'll let you get back to your books. I know you have a lot to do.

Irene: Yeah, I do.

Betsy: OK. See you tomorrow.

Irene: Bye.

II. Analysis

1. Which dialogues are more formal? Less formal?
2. If you want to close a conversation, you usually need an excuse to do so. A few of the most common ones are listed under "Phrases."
3. Do you usually need an excuse to close a conversation in your culture? Explain.
4. Are there rules as to who can close a conversation in your culture, for example, the oldest, the highest in rank, the caller in a telephone conversation?

III. Phrases

Formal

1. *On the telephone*
   a. Thank you for calling
   b. It was nice of you to call.
2. I won't take any more of your time.
   I'll let you go now.
3. Thank you for your help.
4. I've enjoyed talking with you.
5. If you'll excuse me, } Please excuse me, } { I have another appointment. I must leave. I have another call. I have a class. someone is waiting for me.
6. I'd like to talk about this some more, but . . .
7. Can we talk about this another time?

Informal

1. I'll let you get back to your $\begin{cases} \text{dinner.} \\ \text{work.} \\ \text{books.} \\ \text{company.} \end{cases}$

2. I've got to go.

3. I've got to go, $\begin{cases} \text{I have a class.} \\ \text{I have an appointment.} \\ \text{I have to meet someone.} \end{cases}$

4. *On the telephone*
   a. I have to hang up now.
   b. Thanks for calling.

Can you add any?

IV. Practice

A. Write dialogues for these situations. Are they formal or informal? Why?

   1. Paul has been talking with Mr. Shafer, the foreign student advisor. He needs some help getting a visa for his sister to spend a year here. Mr. Shafer is ready to close the conversation.
   2. Sheila is talking on the phone with her good friend about the baseball (or soccer) game last night. Suddenly the doorbell rings. She closes the conversation.
   3. Hirono has gone to the personnel office of a large university to apply for a job. Before closing the conversation, the clerk asks her if she understands the application form.
   4. Toshi is talking with his classmate about which night is best for the class party. He doesn't agree with her suggestion, but he can't talk any more now.

B. Situations

   1. You are talking to your friend, "just shooting the breeze," when you realize that you have an appointment in five minutes. Close the conversation.
   2. You are a professor and you have been talking with a student about his last test grade, which was very low. You're getting tired of talking to him and you have lots of work to do. Close the conversation.

3. You are talking to your mother on the phone and you smell something burning on the stove. Close the conversation.

4. You are discussing politics with a friend of your father's. You would like to talk with him further but you have to catch a bus. Close the conversation.

5. You are talking with a very nice classmate whom you don't know very well. You find it very difficult to follow what he is saying. You don't want to hurt his feelings, but you don't want to talk any longer. Close the conversation.

6. You are waiting for a bus at the bus stop. A stranger strikes up a conversation with you. After a few minutes you don't want to talk to her anymore. Close the conversation.

7. You are a bank employee. You have just explained checking accounts to a new customer. Close the conversation.

8. Your best friend calls. You have visitors, so you can't talk very long. Close the conversation.

Chapter 2

Community-Oriented Projects

Assignment 1: The Supermarket/Convenience Store

I. Directions

The class should be divided into two groups for this activity, with one group working on the supermarket, and the other on the convenience store. Then, in small groups, you can compare information and draw some conclusions. Ask your instructor for a starting definition of each type of store.

Question

1. Which store is closest to the university?

   Which street is it on?

   When is it open?

2. What are the prices of the following products?

   1 dozen eggs

   1 quart of milk

   1 can peaches

   1 liter soda pop

   1 5-pound bag sugar

   1 bar of soap

   1-pound jar instant coffee

1 pound ground coffee

1 loaf of white bread

1 jar of baby food

1 box of Cheerios

1 small bottle Tylenol

3. Can you pay for your purchases by check? Explain.

4. What kinds of drug items can you find?

5. What kinds of personal care items can you find? (shampoo, shaving cream, etc.)

6. Can you buy any food already prepared?

   Give some examples.

7. Are alcoholic beverages sold here?

8. Is there a deli counter?

   A bakery?

9. What special services or products are offered here that are unlikely to be offered at the other type of store?

II. Extended Questions

You may need to ask a native speaker or even someone at a grocery store for some help in answering these questions.

1. What are store coupons? Where do you find them? Find some coupons and bring them to class.

2. What do the following mean?
   a. milk: skim, 2%, homogenized

   b. enriched (bread)

   c. non-caloric

   d. artificial flavoring (or coloring)

   e. economy size, giant size

   f. diet (dietetic)

   g. sugar: brown, confectioner's, lump, granulated

   h. concentrated

   i. carbonated

   j. Nutrasweet

   k. low cholesterol

   l. lite

3. Why are manufacturers required to list ingredients on food products? In what order must they be listed? Why?

4. What does *unit price* mean? Why is it important to read the unit price before you choose an item?

5. What does *brand* mean? *label? generic?* What is the name of the store brand of the nearest supermarket? Why is it wise to buy store brand or generic products rather than products with well-known brand names?

6. What are food stamps? Who is eligible for them? What can't you buy with them?

7. What are organic foods? Does your supermarket carry any organic foods?

8. What is a cooperative food store? Is there one near the university?

9. Classify the following items: vegetable, fruit, meat, dairy product, cereal, other.

   a. Cheerios

   b. eggplant

   c. cottage cheese

   d. red snapper

   e. pickle

   f. yogurt

   g. salami

   h. celery

   i. shortening

   j. succotash

   k. spareribs

   l. squash

   m. tuna

   n. Jello

   o. mustard

   p. macaroni

Assignment 2: Looking for an Apartment

1. Find out if your university has an "off-campus housing" office, or an office to help students find a place to live other than university dormitories. What are its services? Where is it located?

2. These abbreviations are found in the newspaper in the classified section under *apartments for rent*. What do they mean?

   a. util. incl.

   b. lg.

   c. B/R, L/R, D/R

   d. w/w

   e. cpt.

   f. A/C

   g. mo.

   h. eq. kit.

   Can you add any others to these?

3. What is a security deposit?

   a. How much is usually asked for a security deposit?

   b. Is the deposit given back to you? When? Do you earn interest on the deposit?

4. What is a condominium? Is there one near the university? If so, what is it called?

5. When is the best time of day to call a landlord about seeing an apartment you are interested in? Why?

6. What is a lease? What is the length of most leases? What can happen to you if you break a lease?

7. What is subletting?

8. Are children and/or pets allowed in most apartments?

9. What does an unfurnished apartment include? A furnished apartment?

10. What does *utilities* mean? In cold climates, heat can be very expensive. How can you find out how much heat will cost you if utilities are not included in your rent?

Assignment 3: Telephone Installation and Use

1. What are the Yellow Pages used for? What are the two types of Yellow Pages, and what is the difference between them? What are the White Pages?

2. What is an area code? What is your area code?

3. What is the telephone number for information (directory assistance)? How do you find the phone number for a friend in another city? Another state?

4. What is the number for the operator? What services does the operator provide?

5. Name several different phone companies. What are some of the advantages and disadvantages of each? (Look for advertisements on TV or in magazines.)

6. Long distance dialing:
   a. What is a collect call? A person-to-person call? A station-to-station call?

   b. Which type of call is the most expensive? The cheapest?

   c. Many phone companies have three different rates depending on the time of day or night you call. At what times do the rates change for your company? How much does it cost to call Los Angeles, California, and talk for three minutes during each time period?

   d. Are the weekend rates cheaper or more expensive than the weekday rates?

   e. What is the international code? Your country code? Write down your complete home phone number including all codes.

7. Where can you buy telephones? What is the price range? How much does it cost to rent a telephone?

8. How much does it cost to have the telephone service turned on in your apartment? How long do you usually have to wait for this?

9. Phone companies offer different kinds of services. What is:
   a. limited service?/unlimited service? What is the difference in price?

   b. call waiting?

   c. call forwarding?

   d. caller identification?

Assignment 4: The Post Office

1. Where is the nearest post office? When is it open?

2. What is a zip code? Why is it useful? Do you have to use it on all your letters? How can you find zip code numbers for other parts of the country?

3. How is the price of stamps decided?

4. What are airgrams? Are they cheaper or more expensive than air mail letters?

5. Packages are often sent by fourth class mail. What is fourth class mail called? How is the cost of mailing a package determined?

6. What does it mean to insure a letter or package? Up to what amount can a package or letter be insured? How much is the insurance?

7. What is a money order? What is the limit of how much you can send? What is the cost of purchasing one?

8. What are special-issue stamps? How do you get them?

Assignment 5: Finances and the Bank

1. What is a checking account? A savings account?

2. Can you take money out of a savings account at any time?

3. What is interest? What bank gives the highest interest rate in the area? What is compounding of interest? What is the difference between interest compounded daily, monthly, quarterly, biannually, annually? Which gives you the most money?

4. What does *withdrawal* mean? *Deposit?*

5. What is a banking machine? A banking card? What are the names of these cards? Where can you use these cards and what can you do with them?

6. How do you open an account?

7. If you take out a loan, do you want a high interest rate or a low interest rate? Why?

8. There are three types of checking accounts:

   a. minimum balance

   b. 50 cents a check

   c. free checking

What are the differences between these three kinds? What are the advantages and disadvantages?

9. What is *direct deposit?*

10. What happens if you overdraw your account?

11. What are credit cards? What are some common ones? How do you get one? Do they have a yearly fee? What are some advantages and disadvantages of using them? If you pay all charges on your credit card the first billing, you do not have to pay interest. If you don't pay all charges at once, what percentage interest must you pay on money you still owe the credit card company?

Comparison Exercise

Choose two or three local banks. Your instructor will divide you into two or three groups, each one to research the answers to these questions about one of the banks. Then compare information in pairs or small groups.

1. What kinds of checking accounts do they offer?

2. What is their interest on savings accounts? Do they have interest-bearing checking accounts?

3. What is the fee if you "bounce" a check?

4. What are their hours of operation? Are the drive-up window hours different from the regular hours?

5. Where are their banking machines located? What are their charges for using banking machines?

6. Do they have any special services for students?

7. Do they provide any other special services in general?

Assignment 6: Automobiles

1. What are service stations?

    a. What is regular gasoline? Super?

    b. How much does each cost per gallon?

    c. How much does a quart of oil cost if the gas station attendant puts it in? If you buy it yourself? Where can you buy motor oil?

2. Many service stations have a cash price and a credit card price. Which is higher? Why do you think this is so?

3. What are self-serve stations? How do they work? What are their advantages and disadvantages?

4. How often should you have your car inspected? How much does it cost? Where can you have this done?

5. What is a tune-up? How often should your car be tuned up? How often should you change oil? (Beware of ten-minute oil changes; they can do a lot of damage to your car.)

6. If you live in a part of the country with cold winters, there are some cold-weather preparations you need to make for your car. What are they?

7. Do you need a U.S. driver's license to own a car? Where do you get a driver's license? What tests do you have to take to get a license? How long is a license valid? How much does it cost?

8. What is automobile insurance? What are the differences between the following kinds of automobile insurance?
    a. comprehensive
    b. no-fault
    c. collision
    d. uninsured driver
    Why is it a good idea to have insurance? Is insurance required in your state? Where do you get insurance?

9. Buying a car:
   a. What is a warranty?

   b. Is the purchase of a car taxable?

   c. Can you usually trust car salesmen? Why or why not?[1]

   d. How do you bargain for the price of a car?

   e. What is a test drive?

   f. What is car registration? Where should it be kept? How often must you register your car?

   g. How can you find out the standard, generally accepted price for a particular year and model of a car?

10. If you get stuck on a highway or freeway (your car breaks down), what should you do?

11. What is AAA? What services does it offer?

---

1. Before buying a used car, be sure to have a trustworthy mechanic check it over carefully.

Assignment 7: The Library

Note: If you are in a university setting, you should use the university library for this exercise. If not, use the nearest public library.

1. What hours is the library open?

2. Where is the card catalog? What is a card catalog used for? Does the library have a computerized card catalog system? How does this work?

3. Which of the following special services does the library have?

Comments

   a. special fiction / popular reading section

   b. encyclopedias

   c. newspapers (from which cities?)

   d. scientific and other specialized journals

   e. open stacks

   f. information desk

   g. computer searches

   h. special collections

   i. foreign language books

   j. children's section

   k. movies on video to rent or watch in house

   l. records or tapes

   m. smoking areas

n. access to typewriters or
    word processors

o. rooms for group discussions
    or study

p. copying machines

q. pay phones

4. What is the most comfortable spot in the library for pleasurable reading? For serious study?

5. See if the library has the book *The Dance of Anger* by Harriet Goldhor Lerner.

Assignment 8: Local Entertainment

1. What are the names of two movie theaters in the local area? Where are they?

   a. What is playing this week?

   b. At what times are the movies shown?

   c. How much is admission for children? For adults?

   d. What do the abbreviations G, PG-13, R, and X stand for?

   e. Are there any places in the university area where free movies are shown?

   f. What is a matinee?

   g. Do movie theaters in your area offer discounts on any specific times or days?

2. Are there any discount cinemas in the area? What do they charge? Where are they?

3. Where on campus are movies shown? How often are they shown? How much do they cost?

4. Is there a concert hall nearby? What kinds of activities are held there?

5. Where is the ticket office at the university? What is the phone number?

6. What is a conservatory? Is there one nearby? When is it open?

7. What days are the bars open? How late are they open?

   a. How old do you have to be to drink in this state?

   b. Do you have to show identification before you can be served in a bar?

8. Is there a local museum? When is it open?

9. What other kind of local entertainment is available (zoo, aquarium, fairs, festivals)?

Assignment 9: University Facilities

Note: This unit is relevant only to students in a university setting.

1. Where is the university gymnasium? Which of the following facilities does it have and what are the hours they are open for general use? Do you need to show your I.D. to get in?

Facility	*Yes/No*	*Hours*
a. swimming pool		
b. racquetball courts		
c. weight lifting room		
d. exercise equipment		
f. tennis courts		
g. table tennis		

2. What are intramural sports? In what sports can students sign up for intramural competition? Where and when do you sign up?

	Where	*When*
a. basketball		
b. baseball		
c. soccer		
d. football (American football!)		
e. rugby		
f. lacrosse		
g. volleyball		

3. Does this university have a music department? A choir? An orchestra? A marching band? Do they give concerts regularly? Where can you get schedule and ticket information?

4. Are there computer centers on campus? Where are they and what hours are they open? Who can use them? Can students type papers on the word processors or terminals there?

5. Is there a student union? What services does it offer? List at least five.

6. Is there a school newspaper? Get a recent copy and look at it. What different sections is it divided into? Does it contain much useful information?

7. Is there a student counseling center? Where is it located? Who can use it? Who staffs it?

8. What are sororities and fraternities? Are there any on your campus? Do they seem very active?

9. Is there a foreign student organization? How many members does it have?

10. Where is the Student Health Center? Is there a doctor's fee at this center?

Assignment 10: Health Facilities

1. Are there any hospitals within walking distance? If so, name them.

2. What is a clinic? Is there one near you?

    a. Do you know of any local hospital with a community clinic connected with it?

    b. What is a sliding-scale fee system?

3. What is an intern? What do interns do at hospitals? What kind of contact would a patient have with an intern?

4. Can you fill prescriptions at a hospital? At a clinic?

5. Where can you buy nonprescription drugs cheaply in the area?

6. Is there a dental clinic in the area? Where is it? What number do you call to make an appointment there? What does it cost to go to a dentist at this clinic?

7. What is an emergency room? Will an emergency room turn away patients who don't have money or medical insurance? When should you use an emergency room?

8. Are there any local clinics that serve as alternatives to hospital emergency rooms?

9. What number should you call if you need to get to the hospital in a hurry?

10. Can you buy health insurance from the university? How much does it cost per semester? What does it cover?

Assignment 11: Transportation

Note: Instructors may need to change the place names in this assignment in order for it to be useful.

1. Where is the nearest place to rent a car?

   a. How much does it cost to rent a car per day? Per week? Over the weekend? Can you pay in cash?

   b. Do you have to pay for gas? For car repairs if the car breaks down?

   c. Do you need a U.S. driver's license to rent a car?

   d. Does the car rental service provide traveler's insurance?

2. Where can you get a road map of this state? Do you have to pay for road maps?

   a. How many miles is it from Los Angeles, California, to Washington, D.C.?

   b. What is the best route from your city to New York City? Does it cost anything to use this road?

   c. What is a turnpike? A toll road?

3. How much does a one-way bus ticket cost to Washington, D.C.? A round trip? How many times a day do buses leave for Chicago, Illinois? How many hours does the trip take?

4. How much does a one-way plane ticket to Dallas, Texas, cost?

   a. A round-trip ticket?

   b. What is "excursion rate"? What are the requirements for the excursion rate? What is "super-saver rate"?

   c. Are there any discounts for children to fly?

   d. What is the difference between first- and second-class tickets to Detroit, Michigan?

5. What is traveler's insurance? Flight insurance? Where can you get these kinds of insurance?

Chapter 3

Problem Solving and Compromising

Instructions for Problem Solving and Compromising

Read the following problems individually. Consider the possible solutions. You may add your own solution if you think you can improve on the ones given. Decide on one solution that you think is the best one and be able to justify your choice.

Then discuss your solutions in your group, giving your choices and discussing the advantages and disadvantages of each. You must decide together on one solution only (that means that you may have to give up your own solution) and be able to justify it.

Meet as a class and discuss group decisions. *Remember:* There is no one single right answer.

Time limit: Approximately 20 to 30 minutes.

Problem 1: TOEFL Test

Jose is a Puerto Rican student who came to study chemical engineering at the University of Iowa. He has a one-year scholarship from the Puerto Rican government. For the past three months Jose has been studying English at the English Language Institute at the University of Pittsburgh in order to pass the TOEFL exam. If he does not pass the exam, he won't be admitted to the School of Chemical Engineering. Jose has worked very hard at his English and has high grades.

The exam is always strictly controlled and timed and students were told that if they arrived late, they could not take the exam. But the day of the exam, Jose overslept. The exam began at 9:00 A.M., but Jose didn't arrive until 9:30. You are giving the exam. What do you do?

a. Let Jose take the test and do as much as he can before the time deadline.
b. Refuse to allow him to take the exam—he should learn to be more responsible.
c. Let him take the exam and give him an extra half hour to finish.
d. Refuse to let Jose take the exam but write a good recommendation for him and ask the University of Iowa to allow him to take the exam after he has been accepted.
e. Tell him to come back at 2:00 and give him the test separately, even though it is not legal.
f.

g.

Now suppose that Jose has been a very poor student. He often comes late to class or doesn't come at all. He doesn't do his homework and does poorly on tests. Now, which solution would you choose? Why?

Problem 2: Dinner at an American Home

An American family asks you for dinner. They pick you up and drive you to their home. They are very nice and try hard to make you forget how nervous and afraid you are about your English and the new customs. The wife has made a special dinner for you and has used her best dishes and tablecloth. She serves the food and you take a lot of the main dish to make her feel happy. You taste it and you *hate* it! It has liver in it and you never eat liver. She is waiting to see if you like the food. What do you do?

a. Excuse yourself and tell her you suddenly feel very ill.
b. Explain to her that you just don't like liver.
c. Try to eat the liver and pretend you like it.
d. Don't say anything and just don't eat it but eat a lot of the other food.
e. Tell her your doctor told you never to eat liver because it makes you sick.
f.

g.

Problem 3: The Group Project

You are taking an introductory sociology class. You really like the professor, who is a knowledgeable and interesting person. She divides the class into groups of four and assigns a group project. You are to conduct interviews on family life-styles and then compile the results into one report. You will each get one-fourth the credit, and you are each expected to do one-fourth of the work. Your group seems to be working well together, until a week or so into the project. You realize that one of the group members is not doing his fair share. In fact, he is not doing anything at all, but he is still expecting to get credit for his share. The other two group members want to complain to the professor. What do you do?

a. Talk to the lazy group member first. See if he will do more.
b. Persuade the other members that complaining is not worth the trouble. Tell them it doesn't matter who gets the credit anyway.
c. Talk to the professor and explain the situation. Ask that the credit be redistributed.
d. Ask the professor to talk to the lazy group member.
e.

f.

Problem 4: Shoplifting by Mistake

You went shopping yesterday and were trying on watches. Suddenly you looked at the clock and saw that you only had a few minutes to catch the last number 31 bus of the day (the only bus that goes near your house). You ran out of the store to catch the bus. When you got home, you realized that you still had on one of the watches you had been trying on. You had forgotten to give it back to the clerk because you were in such a hurry to catch your bus. The clerk was busy with another customer and didn't notice that you left with the watch. What do you do?

a. Take the watch back to the store and explain to the clerk what happened.

b. Keep the watch and say nothing—consider it your good fortune.

c. Keep the watch. Send money for the amount of the watch along with a letter explaining what happened, but don't sign your name.

d. Take the watch back to the store and try to put it back on the counter without anyone seeing you.

e.

f.

Problem 5: The Term Paper

You have been working very hard on a ten-page paper for your psychology course. This paper will count for 40 percent of your final grade. Very late the night before it is due, you lose the entire paper because of a computer error. The instructor for this course has stressed several times that the papers must be on time. What do you do?

a. Talk to the professor and explain your situation. Ask for an extension.
b. Stay up all night and recreate as much of the paper as well as you can. Turn in what you can.
c. Type a rough outline as well as you can from memory, and turn this in to the professor with an explanation and a promise to have the rest in as soon as possible.
d. Get a good friend to talk to the professor for you.
e. Call the professor and tell him or her you are sick. Ask for an extension.
f.

g.

Problem 6: Loans

Mario borrowed $25.00 from you two months ago. He promised to pay you right away. He still hasn't paid you back and you need the money. He sees you today and asks you to loan him $15.00 more. He doesn't say anything about the $25.00 he already owes you. What do you do?

a. Loan him the $15.00.
b. Tell him you can't loan him more money until he pays you the $25.00 he already owes you.
c. Tell him you have no money.
d. Loan him the $15.00 but remind him of the $25.00 he owes you.
e.

f.

Problem 7: The Bank Teller's Mistake

You cash a check for $65.00 at the downtown branch of your bank. The teller is very friendly and chats with you while making the transaction. You don't stop to count your money until later that afternoon, and then you realize that she gave you twenty dollars too much. The bank is in a part of town you don't often go to. What do you do?

a. Go back to the bank and give the money back.
b. Call the bank and tell them about the error. Tell them you will come by when you can.
c. Keep the money and buy yourself a present with it.
d.

e.

Problem 8: The Instructor

You are taking an introductory economics class. You are getting to know some of your classmates, who seem very friendly. Lately they have been complaining about the class instructor. They think that he is cold and impersonal, that he doesn't give good examples, and that he doesn't give them opportunities to ask questions. These aren't big problems in your opinion; many teachers in your country are like this. You think their complaints are rather childish. However, they are very serious and want you to go with them to complain to the head of the department. You are pleased that they included you in their plans, but you are not sure you want to go. What do you do?

a. Go with them but keep quiet.

b. Tell them you would rather not go but don't explain why.

c. Explain your feelings to them and don't go.

d. Tell them it might be better to talk to the instructor himself first.

e. Tell them that you have another commitment at that time (make up an excuse) and you can't go.

f.

g.

Problem 9: Cheating

You get the results back for a midterm exam in a chemistry class. After the class, several of the students are bragging about how they cheated. Their extremely high grades made everyone else's grade much lower than it might have been otherwise. You studied hard for this test and only got a C+. What do you do?

a. Talk to the professor. Explain the situation.
b. Find out what other classmates think. See if anyone agrees with you, then go together to see the professor.
c. Write a note explaining the problem to the professor. Don't sign your name.
d. Go talk to someone outside the situation, like the dean of student affairs.
e.

f.

Problem 10: A Family Visit

Your family is coming to visit you this weekend. You told your boss at work about it several weeks ago and said that you would like to leave work early that Friday. On Thursday, your boss tells you that he has decided to try to finish a project you have been working on before the deadline. He asks you if you can work over the weekend. You don't know how to react. You aren't sure if he has forgotten about your visitors or not. Your family will be expecting you to meet them at the airport Friday afternoon. What do you do?

a. Talk to your boss. Tell him your problems. See if a compromise can be reached.

b. Arrange for someone else to meet them at the airport. Then explain the situation to your family, and ask a friend to show them around the city over the weekend.

c. Tell your boss that you absolutely can't work this weekend and remind him that you told him about this earlier.

d.

e.

Problem 11: A Camping Trip

You are going on a three-day camping trip up in the mountains. You will carry everything on your back that you need for the three days. Since you are going into the mountains, it will be cold. This kind of trip is called a *backpack trip* because you walk and carry everything with you on your back in a bag called a *pack*. You have decided that you can't carry more than forty pounds on your back comfortably. Now you have to make up your list of things to take with you. Include only the most important items, because they cannot add up to more than forty pounds, including the pack. Also remember that you will not see anyone for the three days and must include everything you need in order to survive.

First do a list individually. Be sure you can explain why you chose each item. Then compare your list to the other members of your group and reach a group consensus on a list. (You may have to revise your list in order to do this.) When you have finished your list, choose a representative from your group to present your list to the other groups. You may challenge or be challenged to tell why you chose an item, so be sure you can justify including each item.

If you don't understand the meaning of any item, ask your instructor.

16 ounces = 1 pound
oz. = ounce
lb. = pound

7-lb. tent
1-lb. guidebook
5-lb. sleeping bag
5-lb. pack
1-lb. pillow
6-oz. small book to record what you see
6-oz. swimming suit
4-oz. soap and container
4-oz. toothpaste
2-oz. tooth brush
12-oz. pot to cook in
1-lb. flashlight
1-lb. rain jacket

10-oz. mittens
6-oz. trail maps
3-lb. extra pair of shoes
6-lb. water container (full)
4-lb. camera
6-lb. 3-day supply of food
12-oz. plate, fork, knife, spoon
4-oz. insect repellent
2-lb. extra set of clothes
3-lb. fishing pole
6-oz. towel
1-oz. matches
1-lb. wool sweater

1-lb. ground cloth for under the tent

3-lb. light-weight stove

2-lb. extra stove fuel (for emergency)

8-oz. spare socks (in case of rain)

6-oz. wool hat

1-lb. first aid kit

4-oz. compass

6-oz. paperback book

Individual List

item: weight:

_____   _____

_____   _____

_____   _____

_____   _____

_____   _____

_____   _____

_____   _____

_____   _____

_____   _____

_____   _____

_____   _____

_____   _____

_____   _____

_____   _____

Group List

item: weight:

_____   _____

_____   _____

_____   _____

_____   _____

_____   _____

_____   _____

_____   _____

_____   _____

_____   _____

_____   _____

_____   _____

_____   _____

_____   _____

_____   _____

_____   _____